DESIGN IT!

GEAR UP!

**Marvelous
Machine
Projects**

Keith Good

Lerner Publications Company • Minneapolis

About this book

About this series

This series involves young people in designing and making their own working technology projects, using readily available salvaged or cheap materials. Each project is based on a "recipe" that promotes success and stimulates the reader's own ideas. The "recipes" also provide a good introduction to important technology in everyday life. The projects can be developed to different levels of sophistication according to readers' ability and can reflect their other interests. The series teaches skills and knowledge in a fun way and encourages creative, innovative ideas.

About this book

One reason for young people to work with mechanisms is that they are surrounded by them and they play an important part in their lives. Computers may act as the brains of many devices but mechanisms provide the bones and muscles that get things done. The projects in this book give hands-on experience with important basic mechanisms and encourage young people to use these creatively. Exploring and using mechanisms gives firsthand experience with important scientific concepts such as friction, forces, and motion. The projects use materials that should be available cheaply or at no cost. The corrugated cardboard used throughout is the kind with corrugations between two outer layers, usually available free from supermarkets and other stores.

An innovative cardboard-rolling technique (page 8) is at the heart of many mechanisms in this book. This enables an easily worked material to be made into strong, reliable working parts once the glue is thoroughly dry. The rolls bond strongly to wooden rods and other parts can be attached securely to them. Wooden dowel rod is useful in many of the projects. As well as the items listed, materials like colored cardboard, fabric, and other materials should be available for use in developing projects.

Safety

● A small screwdriver is useful when making holes for paper fasteners. It should be twisted and pushed through into a block of modeling clay (plasticine). Do NOT support the cardboard with a hand.

● Wooden dowel rod is best held in a small clamp-on vise and cut with a small fine-toothed hacksaw. Adult supervision is needed and both hands should be on the saw for safety.

● Stiff wire for crankshafts should be given to young people cut to the required lengths and with the ends curled over tightly. Wire should be held well away from faces and goggles worn to protect eyes.

● Exploring existing unwanted machines should be supervised by an adult to ensure that enthusiasm does not lead to danger. Keep to small products and broken toys. Cut cords off any electrical goods to remove the temptation to see if they work.

Contents

How to support your structures

Three basic structures to support moving parts

Machines need something to hold their moving parts (mechanisms) so that they can work properly. Cars and other vehicles are built on a structure called a *chassis* (see page 22). Here is how to make three basic structures to hold your mechanisms. Making your own structures out of corrugated cardboard from large cardboard boxes is often better than using thin cardboard. You can make any size you want, and corrugated cardboard will give you a stronger structure. Measuring, cutting, coloring, and making holes are easier on a flat sheet than a box. All the machines in this book use one of the three structures shown on these pages.

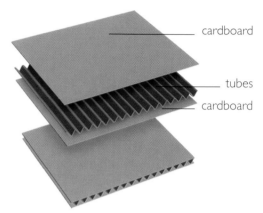

cardboard

tubes

cardboard

Corrugated cardboard is made of three layers. The top and bottom are flat sheets, while the middle zig-zag layer creates tubes. The tubes give cardboard strength. It is easier to fold cardboard in line with the tubes than across them.

Structure 1 useful for supporting crankshafts (page 12), gears (page 16), friction drive (page 19), and cams (page 20).

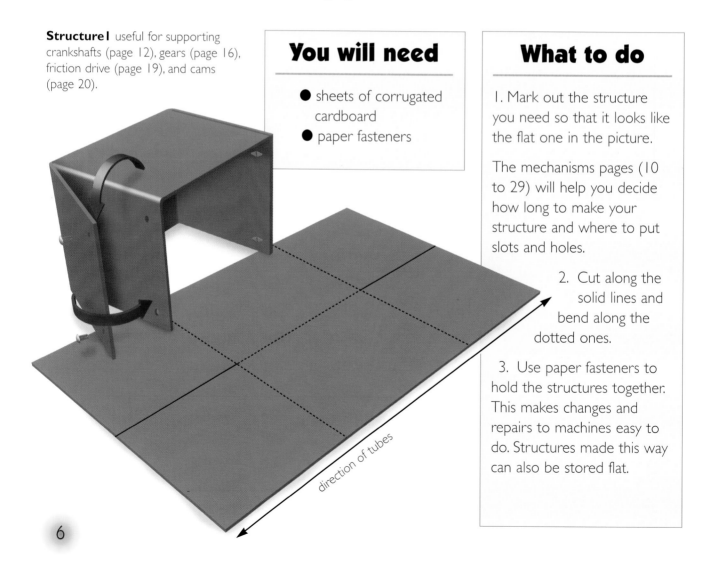

direction of tubes

You will need

- sheets of corrugated cardboard
- paper fasteners

What to do

1. Mark out the structure you need so that it looks like the flat one in the picture.

The mechanisms pages (10 to 29) will help you decide how long to make your structure and where to put slots and holes.

2. Cut along the solid lines and bend along the dotted ones.

3. Use paper fasteners to hold the structures together. This makes changes and repairs to machines easy to do. Structures made this way can also be stored flat.

Tip

Make sharp bends by pressing a ruler on the line and lifting the corrugated cardboard.

Tip

Fold the corrugated cardboard so that any printing is hidden on the inside.

direction of tubes

Structure 2 useful for supporting pulleys (page 14).

Structure 3 useful for supporting conveyor belts (page 24).

direction of tubes

Tip

Make sure the tubes inside the corrugated cardboard go the same way as shown on these pictures. This makes the structures strong.

Making rolls, handles, and guides
Ideas to help on many projects

Rolls made of thin cardboard will be very useful in many of the projects in this book. The cardboard is glued to a wooden rod called a dowel. The cardboard rolls can also be used to make strong handles for turning parts of mechanisms, and to make guides to hold moving parts in position.

You will need

- wooden dowel rod
- strips of thin cardboard 1 inch wide
- plastic drinking straw that fits loosely on the rod

Making a roll

1. Pull the cardboard strip over a table edge. This will make it easier to roll.

2. Stick the end of the strip to the rod. Use white glue, and let it dry.

3. Put glue on the rest of the strip. Roll the strip tightly around the rod. Let it dry.

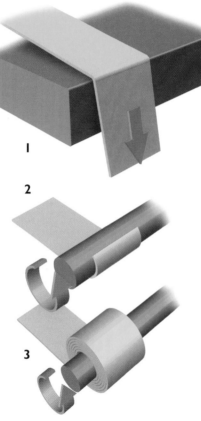

Tip
Don't use too much white glue or the rolls will take a long time to dry.

Making a guide

This guide will hold part of a machine but still lets it slide or turn.

1. Attach the end of a cardboard strip to a piece of drinking straw with clear tape.

2. Put a piece of rod in the straw to stiffen it, then glue the cardboard and wind it around. Remove the rod. Once it is dry, glue the guide over a hole in the structure.

Making a handle

1. Make the two rolls and let them dry.

2. Stick the end of a strip to one of the rolls, then glue it around both rolls.

Getting ideas
Exploring machines made by other people

A good way to find out how machines work is to take small, unwanted objects apart. Exploring machines made by other people will also help you to get ideas for your own amazing machines.

You will need

- screwdrivers for cross-head and slot screws
- a small pair of pliers
- a piece of paper or cloth
- an unwanted toy, old personal stereo, or other small product that you are allowed to take apart

What to do

1. Look at the machine carefully before you try to take it apart. What do you like or dislike about how it looks? What is it for? What is it made from? How does it go together? Notice how parts work before undoing them.

2. Use tools to take the machine apart carefully. Lay parts out in order on paper or cloth to show how they go together. Can you guess what some of the parts do? You could sort and store parts to use in your own projects.

To be safe and sensible

- **Always get an adult's permission** before you take something apart

- **Don't take apart** anything that must be put back together. Even simple machines can be hard to fix!

- **Never try to plug in or switch on** an electrical product that you are exploring or have explored.

- **Never use electricity** from wall outlets in any design project — it can kill!

- **Only try to undo** parts that are meant to come apart (for example, attached with screws or bolts). You should not break anything.

Levers and linkages
Simple moving parts for your mechanisms

Levers can be used to increase force or to change a small movement into a bigger one. A crowbar is a lever. Two or more levers joined together are called a *linkage*. Linkages can change the direction of movement or make a job easier to do.

Levers and linkages are used in aircraft landing gear, bicycle brakes, folding ironing boards, kitchen tongs, nutcrackers, and pliers. *Parallel linkages* are used to keep the trays level in sewing boxes, tool boxes, and fishing tackle boxes. Try to find other examples of levers and linkages in use, and think about how to use them in your own machines.

You will need

- strips of corrugated cardboard
- paper fasteners
- 2-inch metal nail for making holes in corrugated cardboard

What to do

1. Make holes in the strips and join them with paper fasteners so that they look like the pictures.

Important: You must protect the tabletop with scrap wood or thick cardboard.

2. Put clear tape over the open fasteners to cover sharp points.

3. Some of the linkages need guides glued to a base board. Make sure parts will slide easily through them.

4. Try out your linkages to see how they move.

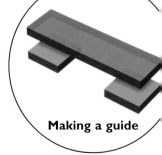

Making a guide

Parallel linkage

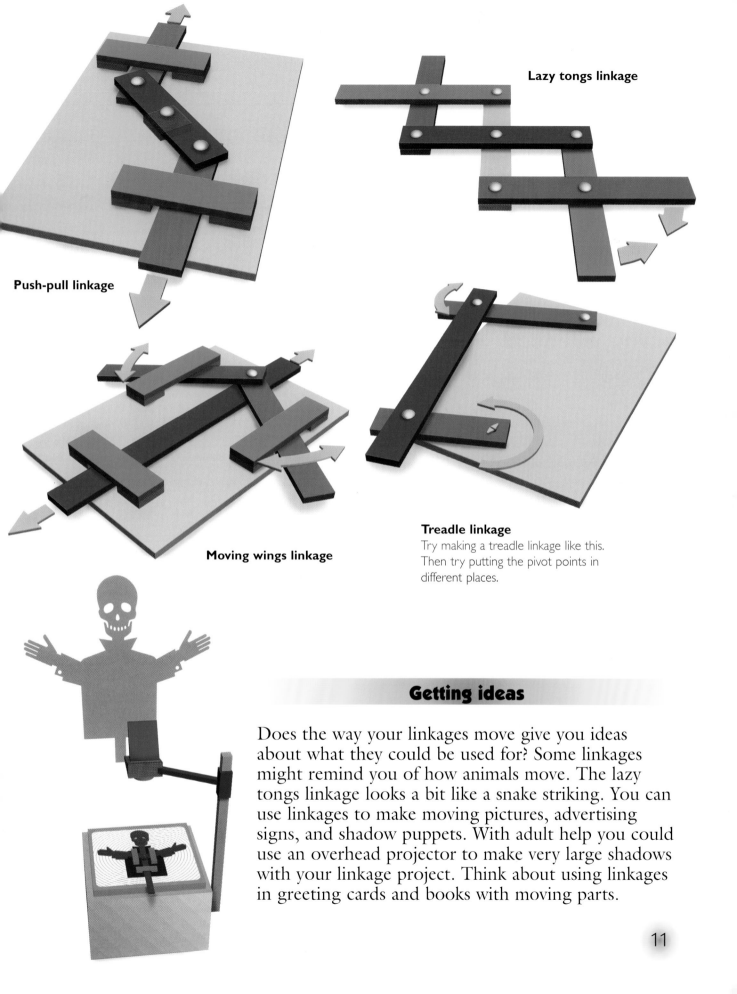

Push-pull linkage

Lazy tongs linkage

Moving wings linkage

Treadle linkage
Try making a treadle linkage like this.
Then try putting the pivot points in
different places.

Getting ideas

Does the way your linkages move give you ideas
about what they could be used for? Some linkages
might remind you of how animals move. The lazy
tongs linkage looks a bit like a snake striking. You can
use linkages to make moving pictures, advertising
signs, and shadow puppets. With adult help you could
use an overhead projector to make very large shadows
with your linkage project. Think about using linkages
in greeting cards and books with moving parts.

Crankshafts
Moving parts back and forth and up and down

A crankshaft is an important part of an engine. The crankshaft changes the back and forth (oscillating) movement of the pistons into around and around (rotary) motion to turn the car's wheels. You can use a crankshaft to make mechanical toys (automata) that will create exciting movement when you turn the handle.

You will need

- 8.5 inch by 11 inch piece of corrugated cardboard
- 0.01-inch-thick plastic-coated garden wire
- pliers for cutting and bending the wire
- 4 paper fasteners

What to do

1. Look at page 6 to find out how to make the supporting structure.

2. Cut a slot halfway across the end of your structure to hold the crankshaft. Make strips to keep the crankshaft in place.

3. Use pliers to bend the wire so that it looks like the picture and will fit your structure. When the handle is turned there must be a gap of at least 1 inch between the crank and the structure.

4. Cut a slot in the top of the structure, making sure that this lines up with the U-shaped bend in the crank inside.

5. Cut a strip of corrugated cardboard, making sure the tubes inside run lengthwise. Make a hole and thread the strip onto the wire and through the slot. If your mechanism does not work smoothly, try to see why.

Tip ✓

It is often easier to work on the structure when it is flattened.

crank

12

Once you have made the basic mechanism successfully, you might try some of the ones shown here. What else could you use them for?

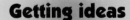

Getting ideas

Try turning your machine different ways and and make it work. Does the way your mechanism moves give you any ideas for a project? Could it be a chicken pecking from a crate or a baby bird in a nest? Do two moving parts look like walking legs when the machine is turned upside down? Two moving parts could be joined by flexible material like fabric or colored paper to make a creature like a snake or a dragon. Could your machine be made to advertise something? You can make moving parts that stick out from the front of the structure as well as the top.

Pulleys
Using wheels to make parts move

A pulley is a wheel with a groove around it. Pulleys are used to control how fast something turns or to transfer turning movement from one place to another. When a big pulley and a small one are joined by a pulley belt they will turn at different speeds. Pulleys are also used to make lifting loads easier. Cassette recorders, tumble dryers, washing machines, and cranes all use pulleys. By using pulleys in your amazing machines you can make more than one thing move at a time, and at different speeds.

You will need

- corrugated cardboard to make a structure
- wooden dowel rod
- thin cardboard strips
- cardboard disks
- rubber bands
- string
- paper fasteners

What to do

1. Make a box support structure (page 7). A paper template will help you to line up the holes in each side. Make holes to hold the two rods.

2. Make a small pulley on one of the rods by gluing disks to a roll of cardboard (page 8). To keep the roll in shape, put one of the disks on the rod first and wind the cardboard strip against it.

3. Make a bigger pulley by winding more cardboard around the rod than you did the first time, and using bigger disks.

4. Add a handle (page 8) and let the glued parts dry.

Making a pulley

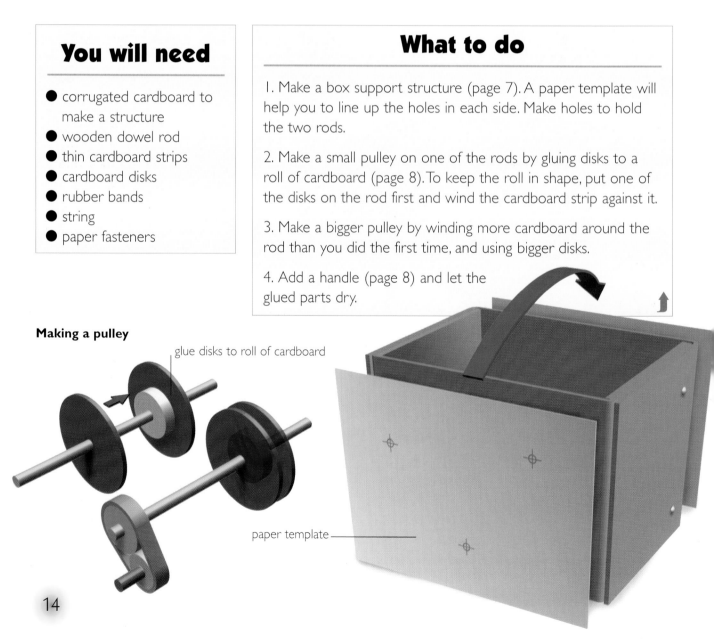

glue disks to roll of cardboard

paper template

5. Wind rubber bands around both pulleys to help them grip the belt.

6. Put the pulleys in place and make a pulley belt with string and a rubber band (the band helps to keep the string taut). The belt should fit tightly enough so that one pulley turns the other. Do not make the belt too tight or the pulleys will be hard to turn.

tie string to rubber band

Adding more pulleys

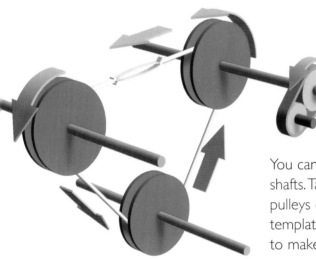

You can add more pulleys and shafts. Take the first two pulleys out while you use your template again. You will need to make the pulley belt longer.

Tip

Holes must be far enough from the ends of the structure that there is room for the pulleys.

Tip

Use clothespins to hold pulleys together while they dry.

Getting ideas

Notice that your different-sized pulleys turn at different speeds. You could use this in your designs. You can use the pulley box open side up or down, or stand the box on its end. Your pulleys could be used to make a picture with some parts that turn. You could add figures to the outside ends of the shafts. You could tape things to the pulley belt so that they move across the open side of the box, then vanish into it. Perhaps things attached to the belt could appear in a window cut in the box. Pulleys could be used to make a new fairground ride.

Gear wheels
Changing speed and direction

Gear wheels have teeth around the edge that fit into teeth on other gears; we say that they *mesh* with each other. When one gear is used to turn another this is called a *gear train*. Gears are used to make things turn faster or slower and to increase turning force, called *torque*. Gears are used in cars and motorbikes, but like many mechanisms they are often out of sight. You can find gears in salad spinners, eggbeaters, windmills, toys with motors, construction kits, and some corkscrews. Look out for gears in other places. You can use gears in your machines to make parts turn at different speeds. Here are three ways to use your gears.

You will need

- thin white paper for tracing
- corrugated cardboard
- thin colored cardboard
- paper fasteners
- wooden dowel rod
- pieces of plastic bottle

Making a gear wheel

What to do

1. Carefully trace the two gear wheels (page 17) onto colored cardboard.

2. Stick the tracings onto corrugated cardboard with white glue. Cut the gears out carefully.

3. Attach one of the gears to a sheet of corrugated cardboard with a paper fastener.

4. Make sure the gears fit together, then attach the second gear with a paper fastener. Turn one gear slowly and it should turn the other.

5. Take the gears apart and stick a piece of plastic bottle over the back of every hole with clear tape. Make holes in the plastic. This keeps the holes in the gear wheels from wearing out.

You could add a handle using some rod and a roll of glued cardboard (page 8).

You could try adding other gears to the board.

1 Gears on a flat surface

2 Gears working at right angles to one another
Your gears will also work like this. You would need a structure (page 6) to hold the gears.

Another way to use gear wheels is to attach them to rods (shafts) that turn with the gears.

What to do

1. Make two gears as before (page 16) and a structure to support them (page 6).

2. Cut two pieces of rod 3 inches longer than the structure. Make a handle on one piece of rod (page 8). Glue the big gear to the handle.

3. Measure 3 inches from the top and 3 inches from the side of the structure. Make a hole in each end of the structure to hold the big gear.

4. Make sure the small gear fits into the larger one and make a hole in both ends of the structure to hold the small gear.

5. Make a roll of cardboard on the end of a second piece of rod and glue the small gear to it.

6. Make a roll of cardboard at the other end of both rods to hold the gears tight against the side of the structure.

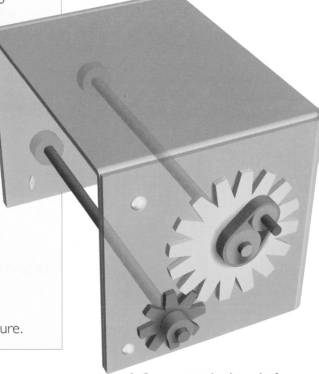

3 Gears attached to shaft

Getting ideas

Gears on a sheet of corrugated cardboard. You could draw or paint spirals on the gears to make moving patterns. Figures could be attached to the gears. Flexible parts, such as arms made from string, would swing out because of centrifugal force. Would they swing out farthest on fast gears or slow gears? Would a small modeling clay weight on the end of the arms make any difference in how they behave?

Gears on a structure. You could tape a piece of thin string with a small weight on the end to each of the shafts. Which weight is wound in first? Could you design a toy or racing game where something has to be wound in? For more ideas you could think about adding other mechanisms to the turning shafts (see pages 19, 20, and 26).

Friction drive

One part turns another by rubbing against it

Friction happens whenever two surfaces rub against each other. Without friction, wheels would not grip the road and brakes would not work. Putting something slippery between moving parts reduces friction. Rub your hands together and you will feel that friction can make heat. Rub your hands when they are soapy. What differences do you notice? Friction drive means that one part turns another by rubbing against it.

You will need

- A long structure that has room to add extra working parts later if you want to (see page 21)
- paper fasteners
- wooden dowel rod
- cardboard strips
- 1 cardboard disk

What to do

1. Cut some rod 2 inches longer than your structure. Add the two rolls and handle (see page 8).

2. Make the upright turning part and a guide (see page 8). Add a roll and a disk at the bottom end.

3. Find the middle of the structure's top and make a hole for the upright part. Position it so that the roller touches one side of the disk. Glue the guide into the hole from underneath.

4. Put your machine together and attach it with paper fasteners. Add the upright piece before the roller.

Try different-sized rollers. How does this affect the speed of the upright part?

Look at "Getting ideas" on page 21 to find out how to use your friction drive.

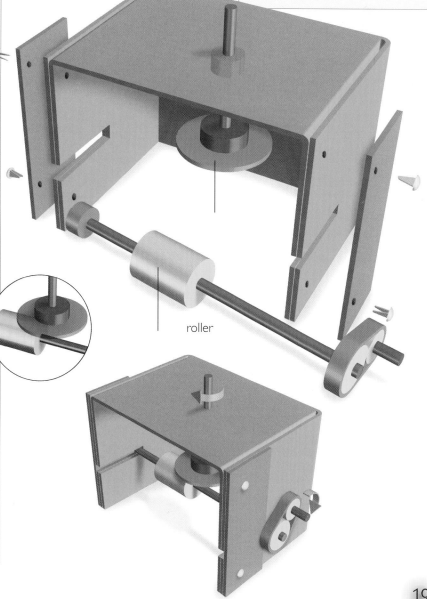

roller

19

Cams

From around and around to up and down

Cams are used to change a turning movement into an up-and-down movement. A cam often looks like a wheel with one or more bumps on it, but you can make cams in all sorts of shapes – even square. The part that is moved by the cam is called a *follower*. Cams are used in many machines. In car engines, cams are used to open valves.

You can use cams to create all sorts of machines, including mechanical toys.

You will need

- a structure (page 6)
- 4 paper fasteners
- wooden dowel rod
- cardboard strips
  - 1 cardboard disk

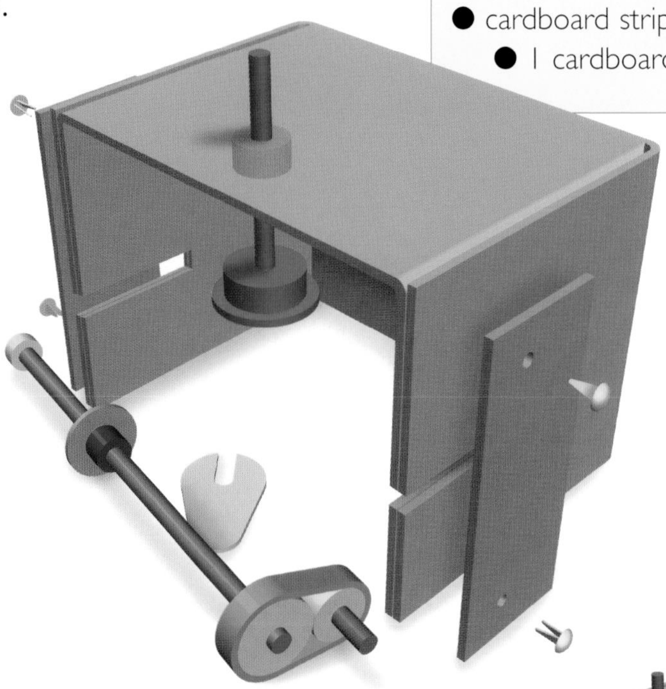

What to do

1. Make the friction drive shown on page 19. Slide on the disk and and glue it.

2. Make some cams, copying the shapes shown below. Make up your own cam shapes, too. Attach them to the disk on your camshaft with masking tape and try them out. Then glue on the one you want to keep.

Tip

A long structure will give room to add extra friction drives later.

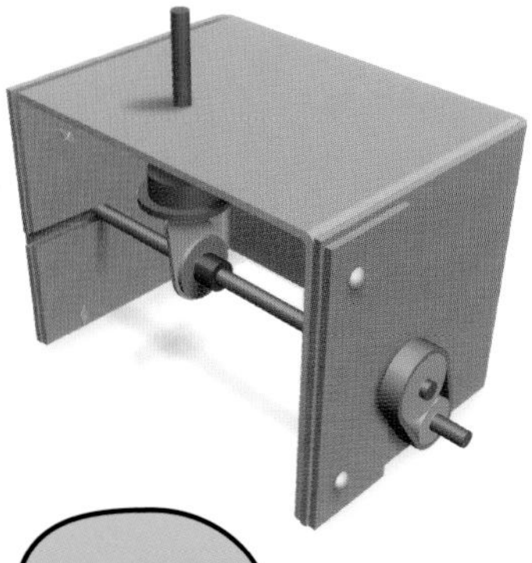

Some cam shapes

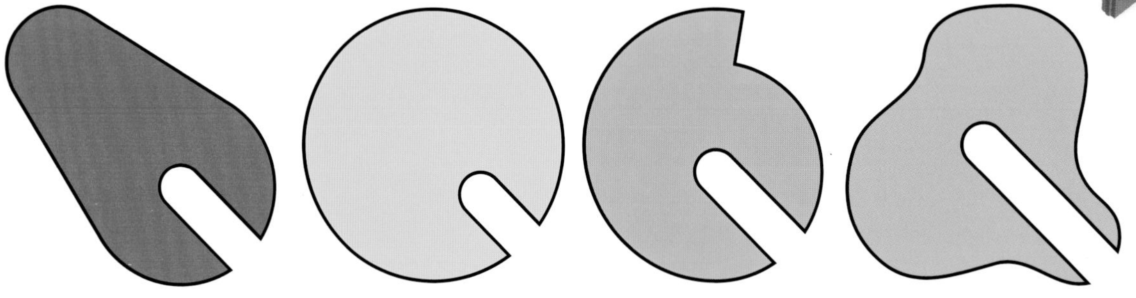

pear-shaped

eccentric

snail-shaped

a made-up shape
(design your own)

Putting cams and friction drive together

You can add extra parts to your machine so that more things happen when the handle is turned.

Different cams and friction drives can be put into the same machine.

By making a cam work near the edge of the follower it will work as a friction drive too. The follower will turn as well as going up and down.

Tip

Undo the paper fasteners and take the machine apart to make adding parts easier.

Getting ideas

Cams and friction drives can be used to make all sorts of machines, including mechanical toys. You could add model animals or people to the rods. Not all the characters have to move – some could be attached to the top of the structure. They could be made from cardboard, fabric, or a moldable material like salt dough. You could choose a theme like "Circuses" or "Sports," or a story you have read.

Wheels and axles...

Building a vehicle...

Wheels are a very important part of many things that we depend on. Cars, planes, trains, and shopping carts all need wheels. You could make a list and collect pictures of where wheels are found. What would happen if all the wheels in the world vanished?

A wheel needs an axle to hold it so that it can turn. The base that axles are attached to is called a *chassis*.

This is how to make a basic vehicle to which you can add your own body design. You could go on to make your vehicle move under its own power using an elastic band and a windlass (see page 23).

You will need

- cardboard for the chassis
- 4 wooden clothespins
- 4 cardboard disks
- wooden dowel rod for axles (thin enough to turn in the clothespin hole)
- thin cardboard to roll around the axles

For a powered vehicle add:
- thin strong string (like nylon kite string)
- thin rubber band
- paper fastener

What to do

1. Cut a piece of corrugated cardboard about 1 foot long to make a chassis. The tubes inside the cardboard should run the length of the pieces, not across them.

2. Glue the clothespins to the chassis. Measure carefully so that the clothespins are even with one another.

3. Roll glued strips of thin cardboard around the axles. The rolls should fit outside the clothespins without rubbing on them.

... and a windlass

... and making it move

What to do

1. Before adding a windlass to power your vehicle, you need to stiffen the chassis. This is to keep it from bending when the rubber band is stretched. One way is to stick on more layers of corrugated cardboard.

2. Attach the rubber band to the front of the chassis with the paper fastener.

3. Tie string to the rubber band. Tie the other end of the string to the back axle and tape it on too. If you pull your vehicle back and let go, it should run forward!

4. Here's another way to wind up your motor. Tie and tape another piece of string to the back axle. Design a handle to tie on to make pulling the string more comfortable.

5. Wind the string around the axle, pull it, and let go. If the wheels turn backward, wind the string around the other way. If the wheels spin too fast and slip, try taping a weight above the back axle. Try different wheels and weights.

Getting ideas

The basic vehicle will roll down slopes. See if you can make it go farther – try adding different amounts of weight. Can you reduce friction or rubbing where the axles touch the clothespins? Would clear tape or wax around the axles help? Could you make the vehicle stop sooner if you wanted to? Could a sail or parachute act as a brake?

Try to get the best performance out of your powered vehicle. Will you try to make it go faster, farther, or both? Experiment with different-sized wheels. How could you add extra "grip" to the wheels? Could you add steering?

What will you make your vehicle look like? You could design your vehicle to look like a dragster or a rescue vehicle. Could you design it to pick up small objects?

Conveyor belts
Moving things along

Conveyor belts are used to move objects, and even people, from one place to another. A conveyor belt is a wide loop of material (sometimes rubber or strong fabric) that is moved by rollers. Passengers at airports are moved on belts called moving walkways. Luggage is moved on conveyor belts. Conveyor belts are used to move many different things in factories, and to move groceries at supermarket checkouts.

Here is how to make your own conveyor belts and ideas to get you thinking about what to do with them.

You will need

- corrugated cardboard for the support structure
- wooden dowel rod
- thin cardboard
- thin rubber bands
- paper fasteners

Tip

If your belt slips, try adding more rubber bands to make the roller bigger. If this does not work you may need to shorten the belt.

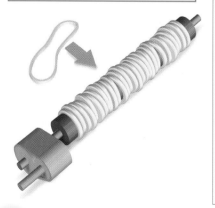

What to do

1. Make a structure to hold your conveyor.

2. You need two rods that are long enough to reach across your structure and stick out 1 inch on each side.

3. Glue and roll cardboard tightly around the rods to make two rollers. Add a handle to one roller (page 8).

4. When the roller with the handle is dry, wind rubber bands around it. This will increase friction and help it to grip the belt.

5. Make the conveyor belt from thin cardboard. Make it tight enough so it won't slip on the rollers when the handle is turned. Use a hole punch and rubber bands to attach the belt.

tie a piece of rubber band on the underside of the conveyor belt

You could design slides or chutes to move things onto the conveyor belt and away from it.

- How steep must they be?
- What could you cover them with so that things slide easily?
- How will you keep a slide in place?

Adding narrow strips of cardboard lets you move things up or down a slope without them slipping.

Getting ideas

Your conveyor belt could be part of an amazing factory. You could design sorting or recycling machines that separate things: a hole in a slide would let small things fall though while bigger ones slide or roll on. A bar over the belt would stop big things but let small ones pass underneath. One belt could drop things onto another. Could you design a game using a conveyor belt?

One player could turn the handle while another tried to fish different things from the belt with a hook, tweezers, or a magnet. You could write or draw on the belt to make a moving message. You could design a new theme park ride that uses a conveyor and slides to move model riders. You could try attaching things to the belt to make a mechanical toy.

Adding electricity
Making your machines do more

Many everyday machines like CD players, toys, cars, and food processors include electrical as well as mechanical parts. You can make a machine that switches lights, buzzers, motors, or other things on and off when you turn the handle. You can also make your other machines even more amazing by adding electric circuits to them.

A switch is a gap in a circuit that can be closed to make the circuit work. When parts of your machines move they can be made to open and close the gap automatically. Here is one way to make an automatic switch.

You will need

- machine you have made
- 9-volt battery and connector
- light or buzzer
- piece of plastic bottle
- paper fasteners
- kitchen foil and cardboard
- stapler and paper punch

What to do

1. Make the circuit so that it looks like the one in the picture. Use a glue stick to attach the foil strips to some cardboard. Staple the bare ends of the wires on tightly.

2. Check that it works by laying a piece of foil across the gap between the strips.

3. Staple on a piece of plastic bottle to make a spring. Use a paper punch to make holes so that it can be attached to the machine with paper fasteners later.

Making a circuit

Tip

Make sure you leave your machine with the circuit switched OFF or you will waste your battery.

26

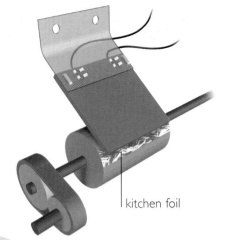
kitchen foil

4. Roll a glued strip of cardboard around the rod of your machine (page 8).

5. When the roll is dry, use a glue stick to attach a strip of foil across it.

6. Attach the plastic-bottle spring to the structure with paper fasteners. Make sure that the two foil strips rub against the roller.

Each time you turn the handle of your machine the circuit should turn on once.

Try sticking more strips of foil across the roller. What happens?

Does it matter if the strips are wide or narrow?

Getting ideas

Could you design a way to hold the battery and circuit neatly in the machine? Draw several ideas, then choose the best. Do you think a larger or smaller roller makes any difference? If you are using a light, where will you put it? You could make a monster's mouth light up or a lighthouse flash. You may need to add more wire so that the bulb will reach the right place.

If the machine has other moving parts like cams (page 20) or friction drive (page 19), can you make the circuit work to fit in with the action? A buzzer could sound when a clown jumps up. Try putting strips in different places on the roller until you get what you want. You might be able to design other switches to add to your machines.

Amazing machines
Putting different mechanisms together

Many of the machines that you see every day are made up of different mechanisms working together. Look at a bicycle and you should be able to spot the mechanisms that make it work. Complicated machines like cars may use thousands of mechanisms, but they will mostly be levers, cams, gears, or one of the other basic mechanisms shown in this book.

You can make really amazing machines by putting different mechanisms together. You could add to a machine you have already made or start a new machine as explained below.

You will need

- a support structure (page 6)
- the things listed on the pages for the mechanisms you want to add to each other
- for the "flying machine": two thin kabob skewers

What to do

1. Choose and make a structure that will hold the mechanisms you plan to use (page 6).

2. Follow the instructions for the first mechanism you have chosen and get it working.

3. Add a second mechanism that will work with the first one.

4. Once your two mechanisms are working you may want to add other things to them, like electricity (page 26).

Here a cam and follower (page 20) make a lever (page 10) work. This could be used to make jaws that snap. Do you have other ideas?

You could add more cams and levers.

Here a cam and follower work with levers and push rods to make a "flying machine." Glue thin cardboard or use brown paper tape to connect the wings so that they can move. Try push rods (kabob sticks) of different lengths.

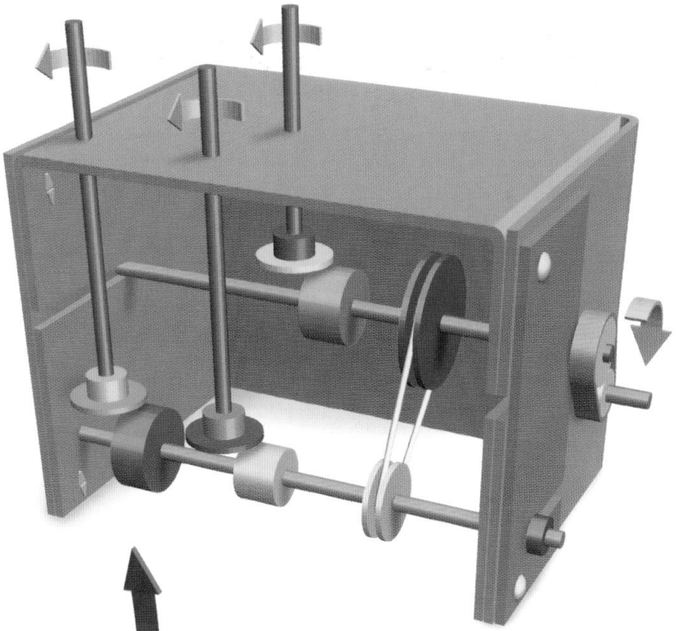

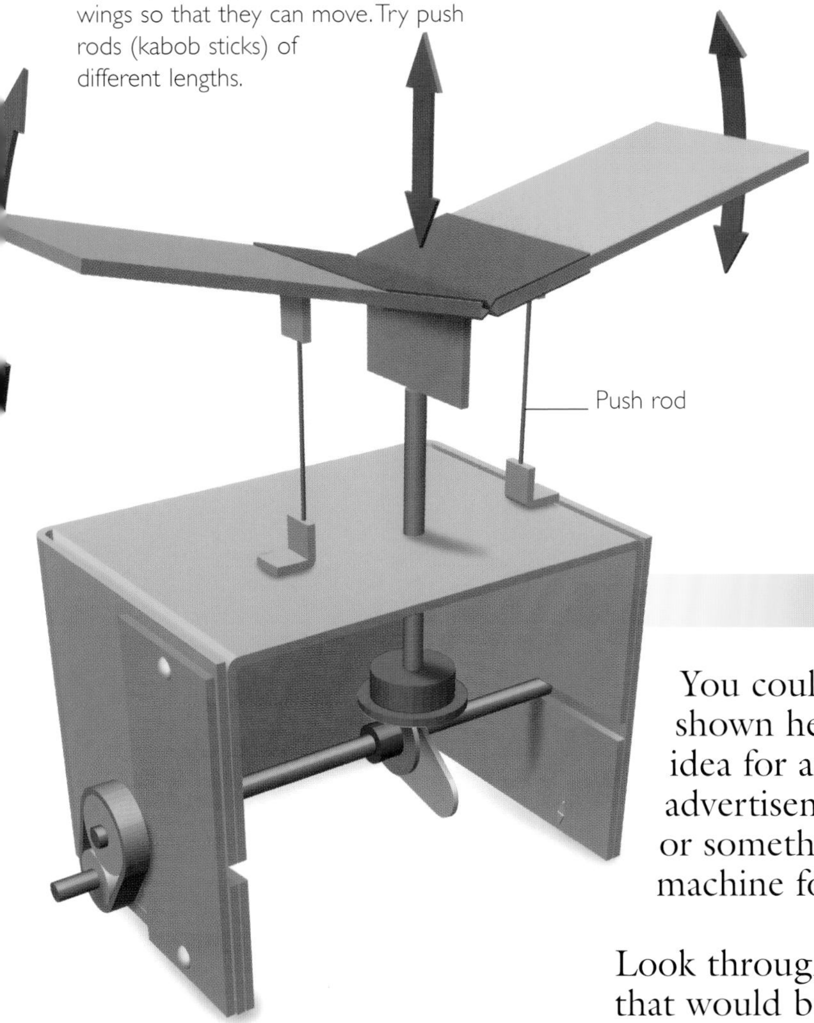

Here friction drives (page 19) are added to pulleys (page 14) to turn two shafts. Different-sized pulleys mean that some parts turn faster than others.

Push rod

Getting ideas

You could make one of the examples shown here. Or you may already have an idea for a robot, a vehicle, a moving advertisement, a flying machine (or animal), or something else. Could you design a new machine for a magical candy or toy factory?

Look through this book to find mechanisms that would be useful. Think about figures, decorations, and other things that you could add. A computer could be used to make signs for your machine. **Remember!** Start by getting one mechanism working first. By making one stage at a time you can create amazing and complicated-looking machines!

Index